Photography Business

20 Things You Need to Know Before Starting a Successful Photography Business

James Carren

For more books by this author, please visit
www.photographybooks.us

Table of Contents

Table of Contents

Introduction

Though this book contains important information, I cannot say that it provides all the information you will ever need. Running a photography business is a complicated endeavor, and requires constant research to stay relevant. Nevertheless, you have to start somewhere.

That being said, you might be reading this for several reasons. It could be that you've been through a general business class or an arts program that only gave you the basics on how to run a business. Or the arts could be a new thing for you, and you want more specific information on how to run a photographic business. Or finally, you might already have a photo business and want to move it from just a storefront to an online business. These are all situations in which reading this book will help.

I'm going to begin this book under the assumption that you know next-to-nothing about running a business. This is not to be belittling, but just because I think that starting from the bottom and ensuring everything is perfect is important, even if you're just revamping your business. Sometimes, a complete overhaul is needed to make a business successful. You may expect that this entire book is dedicated business plans, but while business plans do factor in and have a separate chapter, I don't want to bore you. But I also want you to remember that everything discussed prior to that chapter can be successfully included in your business plans. I hope this will make things a bit easier for you when you finally do sit down and write a business plan.

To begin with, I want to discuss the importance of understanding the business side to photography. If you are going into the business of fine art, your options are going to be a lot different that if you want to go into commercial art. I want to discuss the differences between your options and how to go about breaking into each industry. I will mention how to prepare your portfolio and how to make money and a name for yourself.

I'll be putting this chapter first because it's definitely going to affect how you do your branding. Before you can become successful with the products and services you offer, you have to have a clear look. It has to strongly represent what you represent as a company, and it also has to stand out among the sea of other choices consumers have. No matter what the old adage says, people do judge books by their covers, and they judge businesses by their logo, look, cards, packaging and website. I will teach you how to make sure that all of these components flow cohesively together.

After all of your products and packages are successfully and cohesively branded, you can begin marketing, because branding forms the basis of any marketing campaign. You will have to expand the same look to all your social media outlets, which—today—comprise most of your marketing tools. Expand the same look to anything else you do, from Facebook to Instagram, to Twitter to any blog space. I will talk about how having an online presence today is absolutely necessary, as well as realizing the importance and charm of paper takeaways and mailing cards. I will talk about how to design and maintain both types of advertising and marketing, and how they can both help you grow your business.

As you begin marketing yourself, you're going to want to do market research. Now, of course, this book is in no way chronological, so even as you're doing your branding and setting up marketing campaigns, you should still be doing research into your chosen field or market. This doesn't mean copying what you find, as some people can mistakenly think. It's just to see what your competition is doing so that you can effectively compete in the marketplace. This will give you insight into what prices, packages, and services are already being offered in your area, as well as what new ideas you may be able to bring to the table.

Finally, I will help you figure out what type of business you are. It's important to have all those specifications on file so that you can pay your taxes effectively. Being a responsible business owner is also necessary in case something of a legal nature ever happens.

And finally, I would like to wrap the book up with a chapter on how to continue doing research and how to stay relevant as a company. I hope that, with all these skills in place, you too will be well on your way to becoming a quite successful photography business owner.

Chapter 1
Types of Photography—Fine Art vs. Commercial

So, what types of photography are there, and what of these can you turn into a business? There is a lot of nuance in the photographic world, but I like to divide the business part of it into three distinct aspects. If you find, however, that your work falls into more than one category, never fear. You can always section off your business to sell more than one type of photography. This just means that you'll need to think about the possibility of having different branding materials and business pages for each category. This can cost a bit more money, but if you're committed and you work hard, it can definitely pay off.

Now, let's talk about what those types are. As I've divided them, they are: Commercial, Fine Art, and Documentary. Let's talk about commercial first.

Commercial is what most people think of when they imagine a photo businesses. The most common version of commercial photography business are family portrait and high school portrait studios. Often, studios do both of these kinds of work. Portraiture is always in high demand, especially around the holidays and different times in the school year. With any portrait studio, you definitely want to think about offering photo packages at different price points so that your target market consists of a wider demographic. Think about other ways to make your particular studio unique. What kind of spaces do you offer to shoot in? What kind of props? For senior portraits or beauty shots, how many outfit changes do you offer and at what prices? Do you offer on-site hair and makeup help? If so, what are you going to charge so that those packages are still affordable, yet you are paying your hair and makeup artists fair wages? These are all components to think about, and I will discuss them in more depth in the chapter on market research.

But there is another facet of the commercial field that people don't often think about, and that is the world of stock photography. Stock photography is also in high demand. Just a refresher in case you don't know what it is: stock photography are any images that people look for on a regular basis that can be listed online for people to use legally—either for free or for a small fee. These photos are profitable, because when consumers purchase images legally, either for use in photo montage art or for use in corporate brochures and the like, they don't run the risk of plagiarism and they don't need to alter a certain percent of the image for legal purposes. Using stock photography allows people to access high-quality, professional-looking images with a search bar, so they can find what they want easily.

Stock photography pays well, but in order to get into it, you'll have to find either an agency or an online database. Once you have found one, they will often require proof that your photography is of a high enough quality to be used in their collection. If you are approved, you will join their team. You will then get a cut of the profits and so will they, but be careful. With some places, you won't own the rights to your photos anymore. And though you don't want to do this with your fine art photography, this can just be the nature of the stock photography business. Do your research when selecting a company to work for, just as with anything else. Finally, some stock photography places may provide you with specific lists of photos people have been searching for, while others may require you to do that research yourself.

A third option when it comes to working in the Commercial world is to work for an already-existing studio. This is less of a self-made business option, but, as you explore your options, it can be something to consider.

Let's move on to the world of Fine Art photography, which is vastly different from that of Commercial. With Fine Art photography, the focus is more on you than on your clients. I say this because, when you are a fine artist, people are really paying for your brand and to see what you will make. If you want to be a Fine Art photographer, it's still very important for you to do research on your competition, but in this case, your competition is also what's going to help you in making a name. Basically, these are your local art galleries. You have to look around you, and be aware of your options. It's a bad tactic to pick up your portfolio and go around to every single gallery that exists in your area. Instead, you want to locate them all, and then take a day to sit down and peruse their websites. Here are some things to look for:

- See if they are currently taking on new artists. If they aren't, then you might want to wait a while.

- Take a look at the styles already present in the gallery. For example, as a photographer, you don't want to take your work to a gallery that is exclusively for painters.

- If they are accepting photographers, does your work fit into, or in some way complement, the mix?

- If you feel that your work does fit, it's time to read their specifications.

- Some galleries host shows in which they look for new artists to add to the mix.

- Some require an online application process, while others require that you bring your work in for them to see in person. Others give you a choice.

Keeping all these bullet points in mind will help you in your journey to find a gallery or galleries to represent you.

Aside from just being shown in a gallery, there are other ways to make sure that your work is getting exposure as fine art. You'll want to either have a storefront if you can afford it, or—the more inexpensive and environmentally-friendly option (not to mention the more popular one these days)—is to have a very strong online presence. If you are a reader who already owns a storefront and are looking for ways to add new life to your business, you might want to consider having an online presence.

Before we get into all the details about marketing, what I'm referring to is an online storefront of sorts, using a platform such as Etsy, Storenvy, or Asos Marketplace. The choice depends on what you prefer. Having an online storefront allows you to reach more customers outside of your immediate location. It opens you up to even international customers, increasing your ability to turn a profit and grow your brand into a recognizable name. Because you are more visible, you will also have the opportunity to take on commissions. Commissions are extremely important because, not only are they a means of making income, they allow you to develop your portfolio. If someone commissions you, it is of course because they enjoy your style of photography, but perhaps they have an idea for something that they haven't yet seen in your work. As a fine artist, you always want a commission. Online storefronts also of course allow you to sell the work you already have made.

Finally, we come to the last category of business photography, Documentary. Documentary, of course, means that it is true-to-life and records real events. So, while it is sometimes handled the same way as fine art, there are also some other avenues worth exploring.

If you want to sell your documentary photography, first determine what kind it is. If it's something like food or travel photography, you may want to look into sending your portfolio to food and travel magazines that you already love. In this way, you might get hired on as a staff photographer. If you document people, cultures, or any sort of political conflicts, you might want to look into earning a spot with Magnum Photo Group. This company does require letters of recommendation, but can be an especially good route if you're a recent college graduate. Also, see if magazines such as National Geographic are looking to contract photographers to travel and take photographs for them. With this field especially, if you have connections, use them. (Though this is also true of commercial and fine art photography.)

Now that we have very briefly covered the different options of photography businesses, you probably have a better idea of which route you want to take. The next two chapters are the meat of this book, and first we're going to talk about how to brand yourself.

Chapter 2
Branding Yourself

Every business needs a brand. And a lot of times, the reason businesses fall short is because they either don't have a brand or it isn't strong enough. You may be thinking that a business must automatically be a brand, and while in a way that is true, you, as the business owner, need to do some legwork to make sure that your brand is immediately recognizable and cohesive.

To get started, let's talk about what sorts of components comprise a brand. Of course, the central element that everything should be based off of is your style of photography. Whether you've chosen to go the route of Commercial, Fine Art, or Documentary, your photography is going to have its own unique flair. This should be the basis, and you should design all your other materials around it.

Think about your work. Is it dark, or light? Edgy, or family-oriented? Do you want everything open and welcoming or more mysterious? Do you have any materials or subject matter in particular that you enjoy working with or that occur fairly regularly in your work? If so, can you use this theme as a motif that cane be changed into a good logo? These are all very important determinations that need to be made about your brand. And of course, the type of business you have is going to affect these choices.

When I was in college, I ran into a jam. I found that I enjoyed shooting both fine artwork—which was darker and more conceptual, filled with all kinds of symbolic imagery—and portraiture. I found that the portraiture was much more monetarily feasible and marketable, but that people were also still asking for fine art commissions. Obviously, I wanted my portraiture business to look light, airy, opening, welcoming, so that parents would feel comfortable bringing their children to be photographed. I also wanted people to feel more welcome in general. Now, since my two types of artwork weren't compatible at all when it came to aesthetics, I just decided to create two sets of marketing materials.

Remember that, though it is a bit more expensive, it is a viable option should you find yourself in a similar dilemma.

So what all do branded marketing materials entail?

- Your website

- Your business card

- Your storefront, whether online or physical

- All social media, including but not limited to your Facebook, Twitter, Instagram, and any blog you run

- Any online marketing, such as Facebook ads, Google AdSense, or ads run for you by any other smaller companies

- Takeaways (which are tiny booklets you leave with portfolio reviewers or important connections made during things like conferences)

- Mailers (these can be things like a follow-up thank you card or a coupon for 1o% off your customer's next order).

- Packaging (Yes, this is relevant even for photographers. I don't care if the only physical thing you ever sell is a CD.)

- Your logo

- Stickers

- Stationary

All of these things should mesh, and I'd say you should update everything on this list at least once a year, if not twice, save for the logo, which should stay pretty consistent and recognizable, even through the event of a redesign. Should you ever want to redesign your logo, look at some of the old classics that have undergone a redesign for inspiration. Brands like Apple, Doritos, and Coke are good inspirations. They've changed a lot since the '90s, but are definitely still iconic.

The reason for regular updates is because you have been making new work. If you are a regularly employed portraiture photographer, then you should have plenty to choose from. If you have chosen to work in Fine or Documentary photography, you should still be making enough new pieces to be able to keep all your marketing materials fresh. If you choose to update once or twice a year, I would suggest sending out new mailers to your contacts each time you update.

While I can't help you decide what you want your branding to look like, I can give you some pointers on how to make each look slick and successful.

Website

Let's start with the website. Your website is your online portfolio. Now, it's easier than ever to have a good website because you don't have to be a professional in IT to create your own. If you are, or know someone who is, awesome at creating custom websites, go ahead and do that. If you're like me and not skilled in website design, there are plenty of websites out there that have beautiful, professionally-made templates that are clean and flow well. Check out sites such as 4ormat and squarespace, to name a couple. I've used both, and both have pros and cons, as well as awesome rates and features, and different price packages. You should do some research before you decide, and then once you've chosen your hosting site, you will be able to run live versions of templates before you decide which layout you would like. And if you decide you don't like a template in the end, they are easily changeable. Keep in mind that if a template isn't exactly how you want it, the colors, fonts, even the width of your scroll bar, can be changed.

As you set up your website, consider separating different kinds of photos from each other. If you work in series or types, this can be a good way to do the separation. That way, your clients can easily find whatever they're looking for. And always make sure your navigation bar is in an easy-to-find and clearly marked space.

If you are actively working with several clients at once, and they have requested privacy for their images, but they still want to be able to view them online, a lot of templates have the option where you can lock a gallery with a password. You then give the password to the client, and they're the only ones that can access it.

Finally, make sure that your email and phone number are correct on your website so that clients can effectively reach you. Once you've done your market research, you'll also want to add a page that lists all of your services and prices. Also, make sure that your photos are high resolution (as they should be already), but saved for web, so that it doesn't take forever for them to load on your site.

Business Cards

Think of a business card as a first impression, a handshake. It's going to affect how your client thinks about you, and it's one of the most important expenses you will have. Make sure that all your contact information is correct. You'll want to include an email and phone number, as well as your website url. You might also consider including your Facebook page (if you have one for your business, not your personal) and your Instagram and Twitter. Social media is a great way to keep all your clients updated on what's going on with your business, and it's also a great way to offer things like exclusive deals and coupons.

I find that the best way to include all this information on one card and still keep it visually appealing is to use a double-sided card. They are more expensive, but worth it, because you can put all your information on one side and have a stunning picture on the other. The picture on business card is going to be much smaller in scale than it is in real life, so you want to pick something that is still visually readable on that smaller scale.

If you really can only afford a one-sided card, please do not make the all-too-common mistake of placing text on top of your picture. While on rare occasions this can work out, it's not typically acceptable. And in this case, the picture might be too small to remain readable. So in the case of a one-sided card, I would recommend just using a very clear logo and placing your information in a clearly readable font off to the side or on the top or bottom.

Remember, the goal here is to keep everything clear and crisp. When it comes to picking the design for your business card, I have a few recommendations:

- Whatever photo is on the opening page of your site should be the image on your card. It reinforces the brand to your customer when they go visit your website later on.

- Use the same color scheme on your website as on your cards. Again, it's brand reinforcement.

- Use the same or similar fonts on both website and cards.

There are all kinds of business card companies out there, and I find that I prefer both Vistaprint and Moo. If you choose Vistaprint, you might want to go with the more luxe double-sided cards. These run about $60 a batch as opposed to around $20. Moo is more affordable, and they have a really cool, boxier shape. They also offer traditional business card shape and size, and much smaller ones. This makes your options for business cards much more customizable.

Storefront

If you do have a physical storefront, you might want to think about having a window poster printed that reflects your business cards. If, as I suspect, you have an online storefront, check out what their options are for customizing your shop. The continuing theme here is that you want to have brand consistency, so try to customize it as much as you can to reflect your site. I personally use Etsy, and the only customization I can do is to have a banner. But as with my business cards, I select the same picture or portion of a picture that is on my business card.

Takeaways and Mailers

Takeaways and mailers are very similar to business cards, but larger. Takeaways are often used at conferences or portfolio reviews. A takeaway can be just a larger postcard sized card, but it's even better if they are tiny booklets. You can include the highlights of your portfolio as well as an artist statement and contact information. It's a nice little gift for your contacts and reviewers to remember your work by weeks or months after the fact.

If you do choose to use postcards, I would suggest selecting a variety of your work. This could be a variety of portraits, or a range from a series. Even if people only come and glance at your work, they may see something that catches their eyes and take more than one. Personally, I like to put takeaways up on my wall. It's also a good idea to put your information on the back of your takeaway card.

A mailer can look exactly like a takeaway, of course the only difference is that you mail it to the people on your contact list. Now, if you don't have physical addresses, you can create cyber mailers for email recipients, and send those out periodically. So that it isn't just bothersome spam, you should offer some sort of discount or deal to your customers on this list. If you have returning customers, you may also want to include some sort of a loyalty program. Do not underestimate the value of printed materials, especially as thank you cards. Having an online presence is more important than ever, however, printed materials add an extra touch, a layer of care that digital materials just don't possess.

Packaging

More and more, as I stated above, digital files are becoming common. While you can't exactly have packaging for digital files, you have to know that eventually someone is going to order a print. Aside from what's necessary to keep it safe, how do you want your packaging to look? It could be just as simple as ordering bubble mailers or tubes in one of the colors present on your website.

If you have to wrap a framed piece, perhaps wrap it in matching tissue paper. Include a nice ribbon. Throw in things like business stickers and stationary. People enjoy receiving little goodies like these, as it adds a nice touch and makes things more personal. People will rave about it.

Logo

Finally, you've got a logo to think about, and this can take about as much time as designing your business card. A common mistake is trying to make a logo that is too complicated. You want your logo to be reflective of your business, but don't just make it a camera. Do some research to see what other logos are already in use, that way you don't plagiarize. You can definitely emulate something you find, but make it your own. You want it to stand out. As you design your logo, you might want to print it out at several different sizes, both large and tiny, to see that it holds its shape well. At smaller sizes you don't want your logo to deform into an unreadable blob. Make sure it's a nice, solid color that's going to stand out, and make sure the lines are clean and clear.

Logos are necessary as watermarks even if you don't want to use one for anything else. When you're putting images out on the web for clients to see, you always want to make sure that you're protecting yourself with a watermark. It's true that some very stupid and disrespectful people may try and remove it, but it is better than posting images without it for people to just take as their own.

With all these materials in place, you should also be able to launch a successful marketing strategy.

Chapter 3
Marketing Yourself

After you've got all your branding materials in place, it's time to market yourself. Now, there is a little bit of overlap between the realms of marketing and branding. Some of the tools you're going to be using to market are also your brand. The difference here is that marketing means buying services from someone else to get your own brand attention.

Social media in and of itself, without any cost, is a great marketing tool. Don't underestimate any platform, from Facebook to Twitter to Instagram to Wordpress or Tumblr. It will take a while to build up a good following, but you can start off with members of your family and friends. If you have previous clients from before you had a social media page for your site, ask them to follow you and to share it with their friends as well. This is the old-fashioned way to do it, and it works, but it's slow.

Thankfully, Facebook now offers an ads service where you can select your target market and your target budget. That way, you know exactly what region and age you're reaching, and you also get a weekly stats report from Facebook. You can therefore make adjustments as needed. Facebook will also provide you with a projected report as to how your views and likes will go up or down if you spend more or less money. They will also allow you to design your own ad. Make sure it's cohesive with all your branded materials.

Google AdSense can also help you determine your target market and push more viewers to your site. You can also become registered with Google so that certain keywords bring more activity. Do your research to see which marketing plans will work the best for you.

Your marketing strategies are going to change based on your target market. If, for example, your target market is younger couples that want pictures of themselves and their young children, then you'll probably find Facebook to be very effective. That is where I find most people posting pictures of their families. If you take pictures of parties or lifestyle, as well as fine art, Instagram may be more effective, as I have found it to be for me.

Either way, as a photographer, you don't want to underestimate the power of Instagram as an image-based media. It's a great way to keep your clients and followers updated on what's going on, especially when you don't quite have a new series or set of portraits up on the site. People also love to see what goes on behind the scenes. Photo shoots always come off as something glamorous. It's also great if you have a special printing process. Documenting every part of your process can be something entertaining for your clients to see. Plus, it's a great way to remind clients that you are still actively working even if you haven't updated the site in a while.

Also use Instagram, Facebook, and Twitter as platforms to offer great deals, discounts and packages to loyal customers. I'm not a huge Twitter user, but I think it would be a great tool to give quick, concise updates to customers whose pictures are almost ready.

Blogs are also great for the same reason as Instagram. Not only are they great places for updates, but if you have a particular technical skill—such as lighting or printing techniques—you can blog about these things, which will add another layer of depth and a personable touch to your brand. I would definitely recommend Tumblr or Wordpress as blogging platforms as opposed to Blogspot, however. With the first two, you retain your rights to all images and content that you post, and that's very important.

Finally, don't underestimate marketing that happens off the internet. Get involved in your local arts markets and First Fridays. See if there are any special occasion markets coming up, especially around holidays and be sure to sign up well in advance. It's also not a bad idea to take a stack of business cards and maybe stickers to your local coffee shop.

Be patient with yourself as you try to figure out what marketing plan works the best for you, and be open to making adjustments.

Chapter 4
Doing Your Market Research—Pricing and Competing

No matter how good your branding and your marketing plan, it's not going to work out very well if you don't know your market. After you've set up your website and social media, you're going to have to figure out how to compete in your chosen market. For this example, I'm going to talk a little bit about competing in the commercial portraiture market, because it's there that pricing is the clearest. I will tell you that pricing is one of the hardest things to decide on as a photographer, no matter your chosen field.

The best way to figure out your pricing is to look up other portraiture studios in your area. Look in your immediate area, but also up to an hour away. This way, you have a broader idea of what prices are like in the surrounding areas as well. Take a look at the sorts of services other portraiture studios are offering. Do they offer their space and work by the hour or by time slot? Do they have different rates for on-site shoots as opposed to in-studio?

Some portrait studios charge differently based on the kinds of portraiture they do. For example, in family-oriented studios, charges can go up based on the amount of children or the addition of pets to the picture.

For high school portraits or beauty shots, studios charge based on outfit changes, and like the pet fees in the above, it's added onto the initial price of the time slot the client has selected. You have to consider that this is just the price for the time you're going to spend shooting the photographs.

In your finalized price, you're also going to have to factor in the time you spent editing each photo. The easiest way to know how much you're going to edit is to preset packages, specifying exactly how many finished photos a client will receive. This will also help avoid problems with those clients who literally want every single photo that you take. You could offer five, ten, or twenty photo packages, with the price corresponding to the amount editing.

Then, you have to adjust for the type of editing you're going to be doing. For family photographs or school portraits, the editing is minimal. It will include things like: skin smoothing, blemish removal, redness removal, brightening of eyes and teeth, and overall brightening, sharpening and color correction of the entire photo. You'll also want to give the client a normal 300 dpi resolution copy of the photo, as well as an image for web use. All of this basic editing takes about an hour per photo, and you don't want to pay yourself less than minimum wage.

So, say that for basic editing, you're making about $8 a photo. Now if you have a larger package batch, such as 20 photos, in order to make it affordable to your client, you may want to reduce that price to roughly $5 a photo. Again, this is only for larger editing jobs. Now consider that if you run a photo business taking beauty shots, the editing that you're going to be doing on each photo is going to be much more intensive because those ladies like to look flawless. Assuming that it takes you about an hour and a half per photo, that's going to be about $12 a photo. When you're making up your package prices, you might consider making them a little bit less than it would have been per photo.

Aside from just the cost of shooting and the cost of editing, you have to think about printing costs. Although it is rare now that clients want a physical print package, it does happen. If you find yourself getting a lot of requests for prints, then it may be best to think about

21

investing in a printer. If it's a few and far between thing, then it's probably best to just outsource your printing. However, outsourcing printing is going to drive your costs up more because you have to operate under your printer's prices before you can decide your own.

As you're doing your research, you should look at the prices your competitors have. Let's say for example that a competitor is offering a 2 hour session for $150 and a 3 hour session for $200. Don't just stop there. Look at other competitors. If you find that this rate is generally accepted around your area, shoot for the same rate yourself. Don't worry too much if your price is a little lower or higher, but you don't want to overshoot too much in either direction, because you don't want to undersell or overprice yourself.

If your prices are a bit cheaper than the competition's, this can work in your favor. But if the rate is too low, people will begin to wonder if this means that your product is of low-quality. Not only that, but if you find later on that your prices aren't high enough to pay your bills and you have to bring them up, your customers will be displeased and not want to come back. And if you overcharge your product, you'll have a hard time bringing in business. Keep in mind that when you're first starting up, it's going to take you a little while to break even. Something else that's going to be a great help in determining your prices is going to be your budget, where you will be determining both your overhead and your recurring costs. We will discuss this in the next chapter.

If all of these numbers seem a little bit overwhelming to you, you should probably sit down and make a list. If you think that your costs are going to be too much to have your profits cover them, but you don't want to drive up your prices, consider the possibility of payment plans. This will ensure that you keep your business, and your clients can pay you what you deserve.

Before we move on to the next chapter on budgeting, I want to talk a little bit about sales. Sales can be both a great marketing tool or a downfall. The thing about sales is that people tend to get a little bit eager about them. You have to offer them, but offer them selectively. For example, I'm a little bit wary about opening sales. The problem is that people know it's a sale, but they also see the low prices right off the bat and get conditioned to that. I tend to think it's best to start out with your regular prices and then have sale after a few months.

Of course, you want to have sales around major holidays because most places do, and if you don't, you can lose business. But when it comes to coupons and sales that don't happen on major holidays, I would suggest only hosting them for loyal customers and followers. This way, you get full-price jobs from first-time customers, but are also able to reward those that have been loyal to you. This is why I have suggested using Instagram and Facebook as viable places to give exclusive discounts. Also only host them for short amounts of time. These are called flash sales, and they tend to work extremely well. Just be strategic about sales, and don't host them all of the time.

Chapter 5
Budgeting

Budgeting is very important to the overall way you run your business. The hardest budget you will ever have to do is right at the beginning of your business, because you have to figure out your overhead as well as recurring expenses. The beginning of your business is also going to be the time when you have the most cost to overcome. To help you out, let me give you a general list of costs you should consider as you open your business.

The first is overhead. Overhead are all the things that you really only have to pay for one time, when you're first setting up. This includes things like:

- Any down payment you may have to secure your office or studio space.

- The furniture that you'll need in that space. Determine how many chairs, tables, desks, lamps, et cetera, are necessary.

- A printer. And not just an office printer, you'll probably need a photo printer too.

- Photo equipment. Depending on what kind of work you do, this could be inclusive of lighting equipment, lighting accessories, enlargers, a darkroom setup, an alternative processes setup, et cetera.

Now, all this overhead looks like a massive burden on paper, but it doesn't have to be. I would suggest sitting down with your business partner (if you have one) or anyone else that may be helping fund this venture, and doing research into the prices of things and the companies you can buy them from. Always do a price and quality comparison before you make your final decision. And of course, there is nothing wrong with buying some things that have been pre-owned. While I would not suggest this when it comes to most of the photo equipment (unless you are given the opportunity to test that it works beforehand) there's absolutely nothing wrong with getting your furniture secondhand and having it refinished. Even with that though, you really need to do your math to make sure it won't end up costing more than you think.

What I've found always works the best for me is to make a very long list, as specific as possible, of every piece of photographic or printing equipment I think I'll ever need. Then, before I ever look at numbers and get nervous from that, I like to rank them in order of necessity. For example, if you've had the same DSLR for ten years, then it's definitely going to be a better investment to get a new one than it would be to get a $7,000 HMI Fresnel. Don't get me wrong, you can write down your dream equipment on this list as well, but you have to be mindful of needs versus wants.

After you've figured out the things you need the most, you can start doing research on prices. Here's where another overhead cost comes in, if you want it. If you aren't the best at crunching numbers, then you might want to hire someone to do it for you. Yes, this is another cost, but it could end up saving you a lot of time and money in the long run, especially if you mess up the numbers.

Alternatively, or perhaps in conjunction, you should run a spreadsheet. Especially when you start spending for real, it's going to be very important. Keep in mind, while you're running your overhead, that the numbers (of your projected profit) aren't going to add up to how much you're going to have to spend. When they first start, business are all about breaking even—unless you just get really lucky—so remember to be patient with yourself.

Now let's talk about recurring costs. Recurring costs are costs that happen regularly. This includes things like:

- Rent

- Electricity

- Water

- Any other utilities your property may require

- Regular maintenance checks on equipment to ensure things are running smoothly

- Printing if you decide to outsource

- Any other outsourcing you may need to do if you don't have the equipment

It's most important that the profits you make cover these recurring costs. Because these are continuous and won't let up. And if your projected profits don't cover projected costs, and leave you with a decent profit, then you should readjust your prices. Again, use the costs as a tool to figure out how much you should be charging.

As you run your business, make sure that you log every transaction you do. Keep track of what's coming in and what's going out, and be willing to make changes as you see fit.

Chapter 6
Having a Business Plan

You should take all the information from this book thus far and put it into your business plan. Before writing your business plan, though, you should determine what type of business you are. There are many types, including:

- Corporations: An independent, legal entity. It's owned by shareholders, like the companies you see on the stock market. It's very unlikely that your business would start out as a corporation.

- Cooperatives: Also called a co-op. Basically, this just means a group of people who cooperate in order to benefit themselves. When people form a cooperative, there often isn't a lot of money because it's like a free space for people to come and work and show their work.

- Partnerships: A partnership is a business run by two or more people. If you have a business partner or someone who also profits from your work, your business would be considered a partnership.

- Sole traders: This is a business run by only you.

- Limited liability corporations: A private limited company. It's like a combination of a sole proprietorship or partnership with a corporation. It's for smaller companies, but it gives protection to the owners of smaller companies. This is so that, should the company get sued, the owners won't lose everything.

Now let's talk about how to set up a business plan. You want to start with your mission statement.

Mission Statement

Your mission statement should reflect what your company is all about. It could be about why you started doing photography in the first place. But it should also mention your business's specific aims. Do you have a particular focus? What kind of vibes do you want to present to your customers? What services will you provide? It's up to you. And if you come up with a really good mission statement, you could choose to display it around your business. Or you could keep it private as guidance for yourself.

Resume and Bio

If you haven't already prepared your resume, you should do so. Remember that, for a resume that relates to photographic business, you don't have to include the time you were a secretary at a dental office. Include your photographic accomplishments first. However, if you did learn a very valuable skill at that secretarial job, such as how to create a spreadsheet, then you should include that in your list of skills.

Also write a biography. In it, you (and your partner) should discuss how you became photographers and love the things you do in your business now. Make it engaging and interesting. I would also suggest putting these two documents on your website, so that potential clients can be assured of your skills and your passion. If you think it's necessary, print out a few copies of your resume to give out at any customer's request.

Company Summary

This includes a statement of what kind of business you run. Refer back to the types I defined at the beginning of the chapter. This section should also have a startup summary. Your startup summary is basically a list of all the assets you already own that can be put towards your business. This could be any furniture or photographic equipment you already own (so if you already own a camera and two lights, that's startup, even if you've already owned them for years) or just money that you have to specifically invest into this business. Keep in mind that startup is different than overhead, and anything you buy from now on should be logged as overhead costs.

Underneath what you already have as startup, you should keep a running list of long-term assets that you need and their projected value. Anything that you already own which can be considered startup should be assessed for its value. This should be done by a professional, and then the items should be insured at that value in the event of an accident or a break in. Later on in the document, you will do a full cost breakdown.

Description of Business Services

This is kind of like your mission statement, except that it doesn't need to be quite as inspiring. You just need to state what your business intends to offer as a full breakdown. This means that you need to have a different section for each product and service you want to offer, including projected price or different price points. It's probably best to set up the pricing in a chart so that you and potential clients or investors can refer back to it quickly. This should include the price of every single service you plan to offer, even if it's inclusive in another price. This means photo packages, the price of shooting, retouching, printing, packaging and anything else you might do. Remember that these are just projected costs and projected prices.

Client Base

This is just a quick description of the clients you want to reach. If you've already set up a Facebook marketing campaign, you could use this as a reference. What age are they? Are they a particular demographic? How much money would your typical client make?

External Evaluation

All this means is that you make an assessment of what the current business climate is like. Is the economy good? How are similar photo studios or fine artists in the area doing? This is where all the research you did into competitive pricing comes in. Also, specifically list who your competition is. If the market is really flooded, just list your top five competitors. You could even make a chart of rate comparisons so that you can refer back to it to help you determine a mean price.

In this section, also list your support services. Support services include any other people you have to bring onto your team to make your business run smoothly. If you outsource your printing, that'd be one. If you regularly hire local makeup artists or hair stylists, list them too. It's also a good idea to put down all of their contact information to have in one location. Also include some backup services, just in case you ever find yourself in a jam.

Marketing Plan, Financial Plan, and Strategy

Give a brief explanation of your marketing plan and how you expect to make it work. Include any and every strategy and program you use to spread the word about your business, whether it's free or paid. It's also good to include a financial plan. What further steps do you intend to take to not only keep your business afloat, but to make it thrive? This is where you're going to keep a running list of all your spreadsheets, your profits and losses, your projections for the coming year, and any other important financial considerations you may have.

Team

Who is your current team? Yourself? A business partner? Anyone that provides extraneous funding? Any photo assistants or outsourced editors? Hair and makeup artists? Make sure you update it as changes occur.

Goals

You should always finish out your business plan with projected goals. Use a timeline of one year, five years, ten years. Make sure your goals are reasonable and reachable. Check back in about six months to see if you're coming close to meeting the year's goal.

Chapter 7
Staying Relevant

Staying relevant simply means checking back with your plans and your research to make sure that you're on track. Make sure you're watching your competition and paying attention to what's happening on social media. Introduce new marketing tactics if you see that things aren't working properly or as effectively as you would like them to. Streamline your branding every six months to a year to keep things fresh. Make sure to update your spreadsheets daily and make sure everything balances out weekly.

Basically, staying relevant means that you just need to stay on top of your business. Keep your client base updated and involved. Never miss an opportunity to jump on new social media and new techniques. Add new services as you learn them, and take polls and suggestions from your clients.

As long as you're constantly learning and experimenting, your business should be able to stay current and fresh.

Conclusion

Again, I would like to reiterate that running a business is a constant learning and exploration process. Being an entrepreneur is as much about being creative as being a photographer is. While I know you might have to do some more research to streamline your photography business to suit your specific needs, I hope that this book will provide you with enough information to get you started, or to get you started on a revamp of your current business.

Everything in the first few chapters can be put into use as you build your business plan. In closing, let me tell you about how I would go about setting up my business from the beginning.

Outline your business plan first, and figure out all the basic components. Before you can go about researching your competition, you have to know what you're about. Make that statement, and decide on the types of services you want to offer. Knowing this, you can research the current climate. Find out who your competition is and offer the same services that they do, if not more, at competitive pricing.

Competitive pricing will make you stand out, and so will unique branding. You're running a creative business, so express that creativity and uniqueness and make yourself noticeable. People are always looking for photographers, and the market is flooded with them, so your outward packaging is going to be the first thing that draws customers in. If you don't feel like you can do it on your own, consider it a startup cost to hire a really great graphic designer.

Figure out how much your startup costs are going to be, and start out running accurate and detailed spreadsheets. If you don't start out good habits, you'll have too much catching up to do later, and that's when you can run into problems.

If you come up with an awesome marketing plan, your business will be burgeoning in no time. Use all the resources you have at your disposal, from social media to family connections, to the friends and clients you already have.

If you are meticulous about everything from the start, I feel certain that you will have a great chance at running a fully successful business. Refer back to this guide whenever you find yourself stuck, and remember to update your business plans and goals regularly.

Did you Like "Photography Business"?

Before you go, I'd like to say thank you so much for purchasing my book.

I know you could have picked from dozens of books on this subject, but you took a chance with mine, and I'm truly grateful for that.

So, once again, a big thanks for downloading this book and reading all the way to the end—I truly appreciate it.

Now I'd like to ask for a small favor if you don't mind:

Would you be so kind as to take a minute of your time and leave a review for this book on Amazon?

This feedback will help me continue to write the kind of books that help you get results. And if you loved it, then please feel free to let me know! :)

More Books By James Carren:

Portrait Photography - 9 Tips Your Camera Manual Never Told You About Portrait Photography

Landscape Photography - 10 Essential Tips to Take Your Landscape Photography to The Next Level

Photography Lighting - Top 10 Must-Know Photography Lighting Facts to Shoot Like a Pro in Your Home Studio

www.ingramcontent.com/pod-product-compliance
Lightning Source LLC
Chambersburg PA
CBHW071016180526
45168CB00003B/1440